DewDrops on the
Brown Skin

Anita Powell

Presentation by *BookLeaf Publishing*

Web: www.bookleafpub.com

E-mail: info@bookleafpub.com

ISBN: 9789358313222

First edition 2023

This book is dedicated to my daughters, my sisters, my cousins, and every single person who feels underrepresented but are so tired of trying to fit in. My advice to you is to stand out as loud and proud as you can; because whatever makes you "different" is probably your greatest asset.

So, get out there and be your most authentic self. XoXo BakwaasBarbie

ACKNOWLEDGEMENT

I would like to take a special moment out to thank my mom. She is quite literally the greatest woman I know. She has always supported me no matter how bad my decisions were or how far-fetched my dreams may seem. She has been the most consistently reliable person in my life and taught me how to take care of everyone and everything around me without taking crap from anyone. She is a strong fierce woman who came to America in hopes of providing a better life for her children and she did exactly that. I am so lucky to have such an amazing role model and woman to look up to.

PREFACE

When they won't give a seat at the table, brown girls are famously known for building a whole new table. Growing up in a small mostly white town as a daughter of immigrants, I was taught to assimilate as much as possible. Talk like them, walk like them, dress like them, however when I truly stepped into my culture and my heritage, I felt something bloom inside me that I didn't know was hiding there. I was so proud of my family's journey, so proud of my long hair, so proud of my bushy eyebrows, and so proud of all the other things I was made fun of for and taught to hate about myself. Most importantly, I was so proud of my beautiful, glowing, sun kissed, brown skin.

Rumble

I feel the kicks in my stomach like butterflies so
small.
the fears are seeping in. I want to curl into a ball.
It feels like I'm lost and will definitely fall.
But I know when you get here, I will give you
my all.

Home

When I look around the room, I see my kids
laughing and playing.
When I look around the room, I see my dad
cooking with love.
when I look around the room, I see my mom
working her ass off.
When I look around the room, I see my sister
and her family growing so beautifully.
When I look around the room, I see my in-laws
dancing and singing.
When I look around the room, I see my friends
starting businesses.
When I look around the room, I see my husband
looking at me with love.
When I look around the room, I see my home.

Starting Over

you tell me I'm soft,
but then you say I'm a bitch.
just hearing your voice makes me itch.
should I say sorry or tell you fuck off?
lay a finger on me again and it's getting cut off.
I found my purpose, my passion, and my pride.
so don't even think I will let that shit slide.
I'm so damn tired of being your punching bag,
the one you hit and punch and nag.
I'm ready to start again on my own,
I'm changing my number and breaking my
phone.
You won't ever find me; I promise you that.
I'm done being sweet, done with the nice girl act.

Pride

What is this feeling I have inside?
I've never been so proud; I cannot hide.
It feels like everything is falling into place.
I've never been so proud. You can see it in my face.
My table is full of women, beautiful and brown.
I've never been so proud. My head holds the crown.

CopyCats

5

I see you copying
every move that make.
every single choice
every moment I'm awake.
you tell them that you hate me,
and you can't come near,
I think you're just saying that out of fear.
I know I intimidate you,
make you weak in the knees,
but I'm really just a sweetheart
with a pretty girl cheese.

Devi

You are a goddess. You are a beauty.
You are a badass. Cream of the crop.
You are a movement. You are a queen.
I know you're trying. Please do not stop.
You are a mountain. You are an ocean.
You are a diamond. Ray of sunshine
You are a Devi. You are an icon.
Keeper of peace like I am of mine.

Who Run the World

7

boss babes with brown skin
putting in that work.
boss babes with brown skin
gonna make it hurt.
boss babes with brown skin
taking over the city.
boss babes with brown skin
book smart and witty.

Talia

8

big brown eyes staring up at me,
so curious and pure.
head full of ideas and thoughts about the world.
I thought when you got here, I would truly be
ready,
but I'm still so terrified watching you grow.
This time is different, I have so much support.
I learned from my mistakes and will do better
this time.
You are the one I have been waiting for.

Mama Bear

They call me a mama bear,
I'm strong and scary.
Protect who I love,
I'm big and hairy.
Won't let them get hurt,
I'm heartless and cold.
Never take shit,
I'm loud and bold.
Family over everything,
I'm soft and sparing.
Showing my love,
I'm warm and caring.

Heroes Don't Wear Capes

My dad is the hero,
He holds me tight.
He gives great advice,
He's always right.
I wanted to be exactly like him,
Traveling the world catching the next flight.
He excelled in school,
So smart and so bright.
He never gives up,
Or runs from a fight.
Even on his worst days
I try to see the light.
But I'm afraid at some point,
I'll have to say goodnight.

ADHD

sunflowers, daffodils, dandelions, lilies.
bananas, lemons, and twinkies too.
rays of sunshine, bumblebee butts,
but wait, my favorite color is blue...

PCOS

12

hairy arms and bushy brows
red meat is bad, don't eat cows.
stomach cramps and irregular flow
anger building, ready to blow.
chubby tummies and voices bold
irons low, feeling so cold.

PTSD

I'm here again.
In this deep dark place.
They keep saying that healing isn't linear.
But at some point, it has to stop.

I'm broken and bleeding.
My heart ripped out of my chest.
As if I was 19 all over again.
Crying tears of genuine fear and pain.
How do I end up here
Time and time again?
Like a child regressing I feel like I just can't
grow up.
The nightmares are scary and meds make me
lucid.

Trauma takes such a hold on your life,
And once it has you it never let's go.
As soon as things start falling apart,
My whole head goes to mush and I crumble like
a cookie.

Blossom

I started taking care of plants because for some reason I believed that if I could keep these things alive, that meant I could keep myself alive. Rescuing shriveled up dying plants and nursing them back to life made me feel like I also had a chance at healing and blooming once again.
So here they are, all 20 of my babies by name.

Sandal
Trunks
Monster
Jewel.
When my plants are green, I feel serene.
Salsa
Hedgerina
Feather
Lily.
My counter is in bloom and brightens up the
room.
Mini
Legs
Spike
Ellie.
They filled my heart with hope and helped me
learn how to cope.

Raja
Rani
Tico
Goldie.
some of them are rare, but they get the same
attention and care.
Greens
Cactuber
Barbz
Coral.
I don't know how else to say it, but I love my
plants.

Midnight Snack

hello hot Cheeto.
we meet again.
so tasty and red
can't get you out of my head.
I know you're no good.
Trust me, I would stop if I could.
Why is your serving size so small?
when you know I have to eat them all.
They say you're spicy and hot.
but I think you hit the spot.
the crinkle of the bag, the smell of the dust,
If I eat another, my belly might bust.
I guess I'll call it a day and put you away.
Goodbye is what I must say.

Ode to Bae

17

I am so filled with love that it's oozing from my
ears,
He lays my head on his chest and quiets all my
fears.
I hear his heart beating and give a sigh of relief.
until the sun starts coming up because time is a
thief.
We spent the day together laughing in the shade.
I finally close the book because my happily ever
after was made.

Gulab Glasses

You can have a beautiful life if you just open
your eyes and find beauty in the ordinary.
Once you open your eyes and see the beauty all
around you,
You will begin to feel the shift in the air,
The magic was always there, you just had to see
it.
You can have a fulfilled life if you just open
your eyes and find beauty in the unexpected.
Once you open your eyes and see the beauty all
around you,
You will begin to feel the blessings pouring in,
The cup was always running over, you just had
to see it.
You can have a healthy life if you just open your
eyes and find beauty in the growth.
Once you open your eyes and see the beauty all
around you,
You will begin to taste the fruits of your labor.
The juice was always flowing, you just had to
see it.

Watch the World Burn

The crackling fire is drawing me in.
it's blazing and burning and glowing from
within.
I feel it's raw power, it's giving off heat.
If I was that strong the world would be ashes at
my feet.
I'm staring at the embers mesmerizing and
bright.
I want to shine like that and be so full of light.
carrying the flame in the palm of my hand.
If I say anymore, this book might be banned.

Keep Going

We're on our way to the top.
We're not going to stop.
Our dreams are big.
Worries snap like a twig.
Our doubts put to rest.
We have to be the best.
But when that fear starts creeping in,
And we feel it's time to quit;
We send our prayers loud and high
And manifest that shit.

Find Your Spark

You read a million quotes and if you're lucky,
you like one.
You eat a million foods and if you're lucky, you
like one.
You make a million crafts and if you're lucky,
you like one.
You sip a million drinks and if you're lucky, you
like one.
You draw a million lines and if you're lucky,
you like one.
You say a million words and if you're lucky, you
like one.
You date a million people and if you're lucky,
you like one.
You try a million things and if you're lucky, you
like one.

BakwaasBarbie

22

Red hair and big brown eyes.
Jiggly belly and thick ass thighs.
Cute bangs and lips that swear.
That evil look and deadly stare.
Tiny feet and tig ol bitties.
Balancing act and sold-out cities.
Busy mind and heart of gold.
When they made her, they broke the mold.